FATHER AND DAUGHTER TIME

Conversations from the Heart

By

A.M. Morgan and D. Lester Morgan

Cover Art: J Taylor

www.nsydeout.com

Publisher: 3 Morgan Publishing

ISBN 978-0-615-33708-1

Printed in the United States of America

This book is dedicated to the loving memory of Joseph Salvador Morgan father of D. Lester Morgan.

Special Thanks

Thank you to all of the wonderful people who supported this project from the very beginning. This project started as a series of conversations posted on Associated Content that received overwhelming feedback from dozens of readers. Words cannot express how much appreciation and internal gratitude that A.M. Morgan and D. Lester Morgan share for everyone who has enjoyed the birth of what has now turned into a published collaborative effort between father and daughter. The manifestation of a family's dream begins now; please continue to support 3 Morgan Publishing's creative writing and artistic endeavors.

Foreword

Welcome to "Father and Daughter Time: Conversations from the Heart." These are very frank and upfront conversations written from the perspectives of my husband and daughter based on a love, respect and admiration for each other. The relationship between the two of them is very powerful and enlightening—in more ways than one. In this book, I hope some of you will find yourselves and understand that in any relationship, if people are true to one another, obstacles that seem to hold individuals back will carry each person above the downfalls of life. The book details life-changing father and daughter conversational pieces that have helped to foster an understanding of the true meaning of unconditional love, even when heartbreaking circumstances test the strength of a family bond. In expressing that sentiment, I'd also like to honor the memory of my dad and mom by saying, "Kudos and thank you for the thoughts of goodwill and emotions expressed by you throughout my life." Just as my daughter and her dad express in their chats with each other, my father was a prominent source of wisdom throughout my upbringing. Dad, in his guidance before I left home to go out on my own, said, as most parents do, "You can always come back home, Pewee." (That is what he affectionately called me.) My dad expressed care and pride for all of my siblings at every opportunity that opened, even when defiance led us to misguided directions. My father's lessons in love and survival are why I am the woman I am today. Therefore, never take parental relations and their goodwill for granted. One should never lose sight of their direction, for it is well-paved by the guiding hands of the people who will always love you, no matter what. Even if your father was not always present in your life, I hope this book helps to answer some of the difficult questions that you have often wondered about. Henceforth, embrace the powerful, heartfelt enlightenment in these open and candid conversations. Overall, on behalf of my family; we greatly appreciate you taking the time to read this book.

JL Morgan

Table of Contents

Letter to My Father

Dear Dad,

I remember when I was a little girl how I would spend time with you and admire your intelligence and wit. I appreciate you being there throughout my growth and development. I remember you chastising me when I did something wrong and your guiding hands teaching me that knowledge is power and to never stop learning. I also remember you smiling with a look of adoration on your face when I successfully graduated from high school and college. I can never deny your impact and influence in my life, and together you and Mom have shaped the woman I am today. However, I have made some bad choices along the way when it comes to relationships and in deciding to do something that I know was not right just for the sake of immediate gratification. I have had to learn the hard way, in more ways than one, because of my acceptance of some of those wooden nickels you always warned me about. Nevertheless, I have grown and together you and I have become active listeners while communicating with each other. I want you to know that it's okay that we are not perfect, and even in the midst of our struggles as a family I still possess an unconditional love for you in my heart. It's been a long time coming to this point in our lives, but it is a blessing to share these conversations in such an honest and open manner. Thank you for this Father and Daughter Time, for this is one of the greatest gifts I could ever receive in my lifetime.

Love,

Sassafras

Who Am I?

1949 was the year my father D. Lester Morgan was born. My father grew up in Slidell, Louisiana roughly forty six miles outside of New Orleans. Much of his adulthood he has lived in New Orleans while I was born and raised in the city throughout my upbringing. New Orleans is a special place known for its cuisine, culture, music and southern hospitality engrained in its soil. I was born in 1978 more than a decade after the turbulent 1960's. However, I have always been taught to possess humility because my success is the result of those who paved the way to open pathways for the opportunities a quality education continuously affords me. My father and I both attended Historically Black Colleges and Universities in the South. He is a graduate of Southern University in Baton Rouge, Louisiana with a Bachelors of Arts degree in English. I am a graduate of Tuskegee University in Tuskegee, Alabama with a Bachelors of Science Degree in Aerospace Engineering. Education has afforded us both various opportunities but is not the sole source of validation for our personal identity. "Am I a product of my environment has often been a question lurking in the back of my mind?" I understand who I am goes far beyond my own understanding and takes a great deal of soul searching to understand the essence of who I am. Well, when it comes to writing, I am just like my father, a lover of words blessed with the gift of capturing life's moments in literary form. My mother enjoys writing and is very artistic as well. As you can see, a love and appreciation for the creative arts runs deeply in my genes. My father has never actively pursued his passion in writing. However, over the years I could see the writing bug in my family was always alive and ready to flourish on its own. The place we call home is full of books of various authors and personal notebooks of essays, poetry and journals by each of my parents. Laughter, tears, forgiveness and praying for each other is how my family has survived some troubling times and these conversations are a small glimpse into some of those experiences. Overall, I would like to introduce you to D. Lester Morgan, my father, teacher and, now in my adulthood, close friend.

1)   How would you describe yourself?

D. Lester Morgan: In looking back at my life, I would say that I am a realist. I would say that I am principled to the point that I won't compromise my principles to secure my future. Nobody is responsible for my fate but me. I pray a simple prayer every day and that is that I reach self-actualization.

A.M. Morgan: Wow that is profound. I consider myself an individualist. I find that learning to be honest with yourself about who you are is a huge step toward self-actualization. In my adulthood, I have accepted that I must be accountable for my own actions.

2)   Do you consider yourself more of an introvert or extrovert? Why?

D. Lester Morgan: I consider myself an extrovert. One of my hobbies is observing human behavior and engaging in conversation. I find this pursuit very enlightening.

A.M. Morgan: I am an introvert probably sixty percent of the time. It really depends on how comfortable I am in the situation. The best way to put it is I am not always the best conversation starter, but I will engage in the conversation once it is started. On a team, I am at my best behind the scenes making sure things run smoothly. However, when I am performing on stage, it's a different story—I am one-hundred percent extroverted.

3)   Imagine this is the beginning of your memoirs. Can you write the opening paragraph?

D. Lester Morgan: Man comes face to face with crises, pitting all his capabilities and resources against the brutal realities of the world. This attempt is history seen through my eyes. It is a portrayal of what I saw and thought and did. Inevitably, I have had to select and compress. It is put forward as honestly as possible. I owe a deep debt to those that inspired me. At times, it has been a painful transition but often a valuable experience nonetheless.

A.M. Morgan: As a young girl and much into my adulthood, I have fought with myself in understanding and acknowledging my self-worth. My sense of purpose has been tapping me on the shoulder for quite some time, and I have finally embraced it. At this point in my life, I have learned to accept who I am and once was. I am not afraid or ashamed to say I have made some mistakes. My journey is full of triumphs, setbacks and heartbreaks but there are also some beautiful lessons that I enjoy sharing with others.

4)   Describe one of your biggest childhood dreams. Has it come true?

D. Lester Morgan: My childhood dream has always been to be a writer. Since I will be retiring soon, I plan on devoting all of my time in its pursuit. The dream was put on the back burner to support the family, but the reward for that sacrifice has been grand.

A.M. Morgan: We share the same affection for writing. Actually, we are both writers—the dream is to become a published author. I also desire to become involved in the performing arts again. A few years ago I was in a friend's play, and it was pure magic. I remembered just how much I love to perform on stage and engage with the audience. The creative and performing arts are where I feel my individual light can shine the most.

5)   How did your mother help shape who you are?

D. Lester Morgan: My mother had a quiet demeanor. She taught me patience and humility. She was well-read, and I developed my love for reading from her.

A.M. Morgan: My mother is very reserved, and in many ways so am I. The most beautiful thing about my mother is that she is caring and compassionate. She is genuinely concerned for others safety and well-being. I just love the way she manages to bounce back despite all the challenges in life she faces. All of these things helped shape my spirit to possess resilience.

6)   You are the youngest and only boy with three sisters. What did you learn from your sisters?

D. Lester Morgan: My sisters taught me what a woman looks for in a man. I was taught to be well-groomed, mannerable, well-read and to have a little finesse.

A.M. Morgan: I am an only child, but I have several cousins with whom I have formed strong bonds. Growing up as an only child, I had a tendency to think it was my world until I had my first reality check. Financially, we faced many setbacks while I was growing up, and I had to realize the importance of sharing with others. There were times when instead of having three separate things for each of us there was only one. It was hard at first because I was used to throwing a fit to my mom to get what I wanted but that all changed when there were times when you or only mom was working.

7) Can you describe the most memorable conversation that you recall having with your father?

D. Lester Morgan: The most memorable conversation I recall with my father was before he died. Although it was a sad occasion, the conversation was a joyous one. We reflected on our time together, we laughed, cried and prayed. There were no regrets. It ended with him telling me that it was time for me to step up to the plate and be a man. I married your mom shortly after his death.

A.M. Morgan: All of our conversations are quite memorable to me. You were always very tough, open and direct with me. I used to think, "Why is he so hard on me?" You always pushed me to do better than I think I can, even when my attitude is working against the full extent of my potential. I appreciate it all now, but when I was growing up I felt overwhelmed by your sternness. The real world has been a tough place, and in the back of my mind I can hear you saying, "Don't accept any wooden nickels" as I face daily challenges in my life.

8) What is your biggest fear?

D. Lester Morgan: My biggest fear is leaving this earth and not having lived up to my greatest potential. To be granted life is our gift from God, and what we become is our gift to God.

A.M. Morgan: My biggest fear is losing focus on what my true God-given purpose is. We spend a great deal of our lives chasing dreams and things that will make us happy. I hope I am not too blind to see that what I am searching for is right before my eyes.

9) What are some moments in your life that you would consider to be character-defining?

D. Lester Morgan: College life and military life were character-defining for me. Marriage life and fatherhood were character-defining. In these days and times, every day is a defining moment.

A.M. Morgan: Learning to share my personal space with my first college roommate was an extreme character-building experience for me. Another defining moment was when I quit my full-time job a few years ago because I was unhappy. The year it took to find a better-suiting job and putting my full faith and trust in God has helped further shape my sense of resilience.

10) What is it that you see in me that reminds you so much of yourself?

D. Lester Morgan: I think that it is your energetic spirit and your quest for truth as well as your perseverance and self-determination.

A.M. Morgan: Well, I guess the apple doesn't fall far from the tree. *(Smiles).*

11) You always expressed to me the importance of knowing who I am before attempting to share my life with someone else. What have you learned about yourself that has strengthened your relationships? What about yourself has been a challenge for you in your relationships?

D. Lester Morgan: You definitely have to know who you are before you can share your life. I have learned that you get your good feelings from within, and you do not need anyone to make you feel good. My challenge has been that I like being by myself at times and I hope that doesn't come .across as being selfish.

A.M. Morgan: I am an extremely committed person, whether it's in a friendship or in a personal relationship. I am also a very introspective person; like you, I enjoy being by myself at times. I process how I feel and think about something before I can communicate it to someone. I am an extroverted person's worst nightmare, especially if they are impatient in trying to understand me. For the most part, my personality type is pretty reserved.

12) What was your childhood nickname? Who gave it to you?

D. Lester Morgan: Many nicknames were given to me. Ironically, the one that stuck was Joe Salvador. It was given to me by a classmate, and I loved it because my father's name was Joseph Salvador Morgan. To me, it was very fitting.

A.M. Morgan: I have many nicknames as well, but the one that stands out the most is Sassafras. It was given to me by you and Mom. I guess I am a little feisty, but I am really only trying to make people laugh and smile in my antics.

13) Name something you do when you're alone that you wouldn't do in front of others.

D. Lester Morgan: I practice my oratory skills, which includes a lot of hand gestures and voice inflections.

A.M. Morgan: I am not really into public displays of affection. Displaying physical affection toward someone is a private affair to me.

14) When you looked at yourself in the mirror today, what was the first thing you thought?

D. Lester Morgan: Lord, give me the strength to be what you created me to be and the knowledge to know the difference.

A.M. Morgan: I have to constantly look in the mirror and tell myself, "I will no longer fight me." The person in the mirror is all me, flaws and all.

15) You grew up in Slidell, Louisiana, which may be considered country. You then moved to New Orleans after high school. Did you have any trouble assimilating into city life?

D. Lester Morgan: Actually, I entered college in Baton Rouge, Louisiana. I lived in New Orleans after discharge from the military. The transition wasn't that great because I had traveled extensively, and New Orleans was even more country.

A.M. Morgan: Well, I always considered New Orleans the city. My first experience with living outside of city life was when I attended Tuskegee University. Tuskegee had no real mall, movie theater or bus system, but I actually had the most fun in my life while there. It seems like when you only have access to the basic necessities, your whole outlook on the things you really need changes.

Casual Conversations

A person's face tells a story that can reveal sadness, happiness and pain. It can also bare a warm and inviting smile that says, "I am approachable and welcome anyone who would like to meet me with open arms." However, there can be awkward moments when there is a blank stare in someone's eyes and life seems more confusing than ever before. The impression a day can have on a person can be both astonishing and life-altering. Each moment captures a glimpse into the story of someone's life, love or heartbreak. The people you meet are sometimes a direct reflection of who you are or once were. The obstacles you face can be the result of the painful, continuous struggles that have been passed down from one generation to the next. In order to progress forward, you must understand how much of the past shapes who you are and how you respond to certain situations or interactions with people. Yesterday was a challenge, today brings opportunity and tomorrow is not promised. However, when the sun sets in the evening, it's a time to reflect on all that has happened throughout that particular day. These moments are captured in what my father and I call casual conversations.

1) What makes a person beautiful to you?

D. Lester Morgan: A warm smile can make a person's day, no matter what frame of mind they are in. An engaging personality can take you places you never imagine. A person who treats everyone with respect regardless of their position in life is truly beautiful.

A.M. Morgan: I have to agree that a warm and beautiful smile can make even the hardest heart soften because of its inviting nature. I have met some intelligent and dedicated people who impress me not just with their accolades but how well they are willing to listen and share their personal experiences with others. Overall, true beauty speaks without words through exemplary actions, humility and random acts of kindness.

2)   If you were stuck on a deserted island, what three things would you want to take along? Think of something besides the obvious such as food, water and people.

D. Lester Morgan: I would want a good book, a good pair of running shoes and the knowledge of God.

A.M. Morgan: I would want a pen, notebook and pictures of the things that I love.

3)   You are an excellent runner. What is it about running you enjoy?

D. Lester Morgan: Running is a form of escapism for me. You run on your own volition. Running has given me an incredible immune system—to be this age and not taking any medication has truly been a blessing.

A.M. Morgan: I am still working on running long distances without losing my breath. I used to wear the wrong style of tennis shoes for a long time before getting properly measured for a running shoe. It's amazing how having the right tools from the very beginning makes a significant difference.

4)   If you could talk to anyone in history, who would it be and what would you ask or say to them?

D. Lester Morgan: It definitely would be Nelson Mandela. To be a lawyer fighting for justice and to be incarcerated for all of those years for trumped-up charges is beyond my imagination. I would like to ask him how he maintained his dignity and sanity and not be angry upon his release. It takes an extraordinary man to show no anger toward those who persecuted him.

A.M. Morgan: It would be your father, Joseph Morgan. He is the grandfather that I never knew because he passed away when I was too young to remember him. I would ask him to share stories about his life. I have heard stories about him, but nothing compares to hearing or reading his own words. I am enjoying these sessions we are having with each other because it is creating a history of our relationship.

5)   What is the biggest challenge in achieving diversity of thought?

D. Lester Morgan: Diversity of thought lies in how you were raised and what you have been exposed to. My mother always told me that no matter where you go, you are taking yourself with you. To me that means that if you do not change yourself, nothing else will change around you.

A.M. Morgan: The biggest challenge in achieving diversity of thought is breaking free from the comfort of complacency. It's hard to step outside the box in your thinking and attitude toward people or particular situations when it's unfamiliar territory.

6)   While growing up, I noticed that you had many acquaintances and friends of different backgrounds. When did you learn the importance of embracing diversity?

D. Lester Morgan: Prior to my graduation from high school, I grew up in a segregated society in the South. I learned diversity when I entered college, and it opened up a new world for me. Upon joining the Air Force, I was able to travel the world over. Diversity makes you a better person and gives you a competitive edge.

A.M. Morgan: I attended private schools throughout my education, most of which were historically African American. However, all of my teachers were multicultural, which exposed me to different cultures. I've come to understand that no matter what ethnicity or culture, people are in some way seeking love and acceptance.

7)   What is one thing I would be surprised to know about you?

D. Lester Morgan: I was very shy as a young man. It took college life and the Air Force to get me out of that shell.

A.M. Morgan: I am clumsy. I attempted to walk straight through a glass door once and—bam! I hit my head. My friends laughed hysterically before asking if I was okay.

8)   Name a female in history or that you have personally known that has inspired you the most?

D. Lester Morgan: It would have to be Mrs. Meadors, one of my teachers. She caught me writing many times when I should have been doing something else. She scolded me, but she was impressed and encouraged me to pursue a writing career. To this day, I attribute my love of writing to her.

A.M. Morgan: My mother because she is always praying to God for my security and well-being. I think she is the most compassionate person I have ever known. She always says to me, "I hope and pray all of your dreams come true." Her words keep me going when I think my dreams are dying and will never be fulfilled.

9)   Name five things that annoy you.

D. Lester Morgan: Loud and boisterous people, pretentious people, grandiose people and the use of non-standard English and illiteracy.

A.M. Morgan: Disrespectfulness, arrogance, dictatorship and cheeky and judgmental people who are the carbon copy of the people they are judging.

10)   What are you most vain about?

D. Lester Morgan: I am most vain about my wardrobe. I think fine clothes are a part of what makes a man.

A.M. Morgan: I am most vain about my teeth. I remember when my tooth chipped—it was like the end of the world for me. My friends thought I was making a big deal out of nothing, but it was a real crisis for me until I could go to the dentist to get it fixed.

11)   What are you most shy about?

D. Lester Morgan: I am most shy about sharing my vulnerability with others.

A.M. Morgan: I am most shy about talking about my personal accomplishments. In general, you won't hear me talking about myself in most conversations.

12)   When are you happiest?

D. Lester Morgan: I am most happy at home and with family engaged in conversation. It also helps to know that one is financially secure.

A.M. Morgan: I am happiest in small and intimate settings with family and friends, having dinner or a good time. Also, I am happy when I am listening to good music; it is very therapeutic to me.

13)   What is your most treasured possession?

D. Lester Morgan: My most treasured possession is my education. Looking back at life, I can truly say a mind is a terrible thing to waste.

A.M. Morgan: My most treasured possession is the gift of life and waking up each day with the opportunity to fulfill my dreams and help others along the way.

14)   Why did you decide to join the military? What was the mental and physical preparation like? Did life in the military help you discover anything about yourself or the world we live in?

D. Lester Morgan: I joined the military to take advantage of the GI Bill for college tuition and to purchase a home. It was also a form of escapism for me. The mental and physical preparation was just what I needed. I discovered toughness in me that I didn't know existed and that all of the people of the world want to be free.

A.M. Morgan: I admire you for joining the military. It is something I don't think I have the courage or strength to do.

15) What is the one thing you would have liked to ask your father about his life? Is there anything that you wish you would have said to him?

D. Lester Morgan: I would like to have asked him how he went through life without showing any outward pain or remorse, only perseverance. Those were some hard times.

A.M. Morgan: Throughout this book, I am saying and asking you all the things that were in the back of my mind. As I have said before, I never had a chance to know your father because he died when I was really young so, I am getting to know him through you.

The Importance of a Father and Daughter Bond

My father is the first man that I ever adored. He is also the first man I had to wholeheartedly learn to love unconditionally to set the foundation for the success of my future relationships. I now understand that many things that I held as truth about the responsibilities of a father are based on ideals and false perceptions of manhood. A friend of mine once told me how much she longed to feel the presence of her father in her life to teach her how to identify the true essence of a man and how he should treat a woman. I found myself at a loss for words because I couldn't imagine not being able to communicate with my father on just about anything I am inquisitive about. The father and daughter bond that we share is profound, and through it all we have been able to restore broken pieces of it by engaging in a fascinating journey towards self-discovery.

1) Why do you think it is so important for a daughter to have a relationship with her father?

D. Lester Morgan: A daughter gets her first look at what it takes to be a man from her father as well as the way a man should conduct himself. Her father sets boundaries and helps her navigate the many pitfalls of life.

A.M. Morgan: The relationship a daughter has with her father has a lasting impact on her life. His direct influence orders her steps in her future relationships and life experiences. You provided me with the insight to separate what I expect a man to be from allowing him to reveal himself in his true nature without immediate judgment.

2)   The unfortunate reality in our world is that many people grow up with the absence of a father or mother. How would you describe the importance of having both parents actively present in your life?

D. Lester Morgan: Parents are ordained by God. It is their duty to teach and guide. With both parents in my life, failure was never an option. I developed from them the tools necessary to survive, and to this day I still reflect on their teaching.

A.M. Morgan: My parents provided me with unique perspectives of living in this world as a man and a woman. There are a lot of things my father taught me that my mother did not necessarily understand and vice versa. I am grateful for my parents' guiding hands throughout my life.

3)   How did being a father change you?

D. Lester Morgan: Your birth really changed my life. At that time, I was out of control. I was still licking my wounds from the military and had very little direction or concern. Your mother saw something in me that I couldn't see in myself. It made me reassess my life and commitment to your mother and I embraced marriage. I realized I had to be the go-to person if we were to succeed as a family. Until this day, I am still trying to live up to that commitment.

A.M. Morgan: I once read Sidney Poitier's *The Measure of a Man* and he mentions that part of the role of a father is just being there, no matter how imperfect you are. He said one of the things his daughters appreciated the most was his continual presence. So, I say thank you for being there for me throughout my growth and development.

4)   What is the greatest lesson your father taught you?

D. Lester Morgan: My father taught me to be a gentleman and to treat everyone with respect. I would say that the way that he lived was an example for me to emulate.

A.M. Morgan: The greatest lesson you have taught me is to always seek truth and knowledge. I am always in the state of learning and acquiring wisdom from those who have gone before me. I also learned to command respect, but to also give it in return.

5)   It is often said that women search for a mate that shares the same characteristics of her father, or one to fill the void from the absence of a father. Do you think men search for someone similar to their mother in a mate? If so, in what ways?

D. Lester Morgan: In some ways I do. I think that some men have basically been spoiled. Their nurturing sometimes causes them to take their mate for granted and as a mother-replacement. This can cause conflict in the marriage, especially if he is a momma's boy and his wife is treated secondary.

A.M. Morgan: There are some men who are used to being extremely pampered but don't want to reciprocate. If you want to be treated like a king, then you must treat your significant other like a queen. A man should love and honor his mother. He can seek guidance from her but final decisions regarding his personal relationships should be made between him and the person he is involved with.

6)   What is your advice to a new father?

D. Lester Morgan: My advice to a new father is to give great consideration before assuming that role. Any man can father a child, but it takes a special person to rear and nurture that child. We are all imitators of somebody, so be a good role model.

A.M. Morgan: The best advice I can give to a new father is to show up, not only when you are right, but also when you are dead wrong. As father and daughter, we have had our share of disagreements, but I can honestly say you were always there. I am so proud to say that I never had to wonder if you cared about my well-being because you always provided me with guidance and support.

7)   We have had some difficult times as a family, but throughout it all you never abandoned us. What made you stay? What are your words of encouragement to fathers who feel like leaving would be better than staying with their families?

D. Lester Morgan: Abandonment has never crossed my mind. I have always wanted a family, and I think that ours was ordained by God. For fathers who consider leaving, I would like to say that you can accomplish more as a core unit than individually. Tough times don't last but tough guys do.

A.M. Morgan: Don't get caught up in defining your manhood by external things. Your children need you and understand the extraordinary impact of your presence. Abandonment hurts and destroys the value of trust for a child who will later try to define who they are in the absence of a father.

8) What did you notice most about the interaction between your father and your sisters? What source of inspiration was that to you in raising me?

D. Lester Morgan: My father was well-respected by my sisters because he was always in their lives and very visible. That inspired me in wanting the best for you and establishing a firm commitment.

A.M. Morgan: I can tell he raised my aunts to be very strong women who demand respect. You are the youngest and only boy—I can tell the admiration you all have for each other and how much they are willing to go the extra mile in helping you understand the importance of the women who helped to shape your life.

9) What did raising me teach you about women that you may have not previously appreciated as it relates to the communication between men and women?

D. Lester Morgan: Raising you taught me to be more sensitive toward open communication. I have shared conversations with you and ventured into areas of expression that were never asked before by any woman, including your mother.

A.M. Morgan: Communication—what more can I say—it is the nucleus of all relationships, both personal and professional. These conversations have definitely helped to not only restore our relationship but also are a blueprint for me in strengthening my future relationships.

10) What is a father's greatest fear in regard to his daughter venturing into the world on her own?

D. Lester Morgan: My greatest fear has been you choosing the right mate. I can't make that choice for you, but it is my hope and prayer that you follow your heart. Nevertheless, you have shown me that you can adapt, and your decisions have been sound.

A.M. Morgan: I don't know what the future holds, and I cannot predict what my lifelong mate will be like. It is my hope that we are able to communicate openly with each other and equally able to confront each other about problems instead of speaking through other people. Overall, at the end of the day I just want to be loved and respected, and I am willing to give just as much as I expect from someone else.

11) What has been the biggest difference in communicating with me as a young girl verses an adult woman? What has remained the same?

D. Lester Morgan: Conversations with you have been easier because I reared you and we share some of the same values. Adult women come with their own upbringing and value system that sometimes clashes with others. It remains the same that women want honesty and commitment in a relationship, and my experience communicating with you is further confirmation of that.

A.M. Morgan: Conversations with you earlier in my life were very stern and commanding, especially in terms of you guiding me on the difficulties of life. Now our conversations are more relaxed in open dialogue that fosters discovering and understanding our strengths and conquering some of our weaknesses. I feel like a sponge sometimes because I am soaking up all of the life lessons you are sharing with me and getting to know D. Lester Morgan—the man, not just my father.

12) Mom said that when I was a little baby you held me high in the sky as she watched from the kitchen window in awe. Do you remember what you were feeling at that moment?

D. Lester Morgan: I recall that I had always wanted a daughter. To be blessed with your birth was truly a sign from God. Cradling you in my arms made me realize that it was no longer about me. Your birth made me reassess my life and make some major decisions. Holding you up to the sky was me giving praise. I knew from the beginning that you were an extraordinary child.

A.M. Morgan: I feel like you are always holding me up as I set out to fulfill my dreams and face some disappointments. Life has definitely dealt me some difficult cards to play, but your encouraging words are always on my mind when adversity presents itself.

13) How would your parenting style have been different if you had a son?

D. Lester Morgan: I have pondered that thought before. In looking at the young men today, I am sure it would have been a challenge. Nevertheless, I don't think that my style would have changed dramatically. The main thing is to lead by example and not try to dictate.

A.M. Morgan: I always thought you were being extra hard on me, as if I was not a girl, so to speak. I can say that you were always brutally honest with me on what to expect in what is often perceived as a man's world.

14) What is the best advice you can give to me in regard to raising children of my own?

D. Lester Morgan: Be ready mentally before embracing motherhood and within the confines of marriage. You won't truly understand motherhood until you experience it. Don't aspire to be a single parent because it is a huge and difficult undertaking.

A.M. Morgan: Thank you for that advice. My biggest fear in raising children of my own is that I won't always be the best role model to them. Children are like sponges—they soak up everything you say and do. I do believe that a person should not deliberately try to raise a child alone. However, sometimes due to circumstances beyond a person's control, raising children alone becomes a reality.

15) Do you think sexism supersedes racism in America? Why or why not?

D. Lester Morgan: It is my belief that racism and sexism intersect and both are deeply woven and entrenched into the very fibers of the founding of this country. Gender and racial equality should be non-negotiable.

A.M. Morgan: I must admit I have often asked myself if someone sees the content of my character first or simply defines me by race and gender. Working in the engineering field, there are often more males than females, and there are still some misconceptions regarding the perceived role of a woman.

16) Imagine you are teaching a seminar to young girls about the importance of self-respect. What would be three of the most important key points that you would bring up in the discussion?

D. Lester Morgan: 1) Respect yourself, if no one else. 2) Earn respect by being a good example for others to emulate. 3) Be an individual and don't conform to standards imposed by others.

A.M. Morgan: Young ladies, you are beautiful and every time you wake up in the morning remember these three things: 1) Smile, don't you know God loves you? 2) Never define your beauty based on someone else's ideals because they are always subject to change. 3) Its never too late to succeed, but never compromise yourself in order to do so.

Reflections on Manhood

I can honestly say that as I grew as a young woman, I was selfish in my thinking because never did it occur to me that my father or men in general, are vulnerable and self-conscious. As an adolescent and young adult, I never saw a man cry or openly express emotions. My father was intelligent, hardworking and dedicated, but I never saw him physically shed a tear. As a result, I have contemplated endlessly on why it seems that women are emotional creatures and men are masters of withholding their emotions. I've come to understand that it's not that men don't have feelings, but that they have a tendency to react in a more indirect manner. The male ego is very fragile, and sometimes pride is his greatest possession. The American myth that men who express themselves are weak is also a contributing factor. Today, I have opened my mind and decided to have an intimate discussion with my father on reflections of manhood.

1) How did you gain an understanding of the definition of manhood, and how was your transition into accepting all of the responsibilities that come along with it?

D. Lester Morgan: In growing up, I was taught that a man is supposed to be a provider. This meant getting an education and finding a good job. I was never taught the spiritual aspects of being a man. Later years taught me that in order to grow holistically, spirituality must be a part of it.

A.M. Morgan: That is very profound. I have now come to understand that men often battle with fulfilling society's definition of manhood and with trying to discover their own sense of well-being.

2) Describe the men that had the most impact in your life from childhood to adulthood.

D. Lester Morgan: All of the neighborhood men had a great impact on my life. When I was growing up, there were very few single-parent households. If there was, any man stepped up to the plate and assumed that role if he saw the need. My father had the greatest impact on my life. He led by example and although he was stern, there was compassion. To this day, I try to pattern my life after him.

A.M. Morgan: Of course, you had the biggest impact on my life from childhood to my early adulthood. You were always very open and honest with me and didn't withhold harsh truths on what to expect in the real world. In my adulthood, I have also had many male friends whom I cherish dearly for helping me understand the male perspective. I know many believe men and women can't be friends but I say, "Have you really tried to embrace the idea?"

3) What moment or moments defined your entrance into manhood?

D. Lester Morgan: Entering College and going to the military defined my entrance into manhood. Those were turbulent times of the sixties. It was a period of bewilderment and escapism. However, I think that period helped shape my life definitively.

A.M. Morgan: Wow, sounds like a separate conversation in a different book. Defining the entrance into manhood is much more complex than I ever imagined.

4)   What would you do if you were the opposite gender for a day?

D. Lester Morgan: I would attempt to understand the needs of a woman and how she balances the many demands of womanhood. I think the world in general disrespects a woman's worth, and this has been one of its downfalls.

A.M. Morgan: I would like to hang with the boys to hear what men really talk about behind closed doors. I think these conversations we've been having have definitely helped me understand what men really think about various aspects of life.

5)   Marvin Gaye is one of your favorite singers. Do you feel a connection with him through his music? What songs of his impressive collection of music do you think outline your life as a male and why?

D. Lester Morgan: "What's Going On?" is my favorite song by Marvin Gaye; it chronicles my life during the sixties, my four-year military stint and my return home. Marvin's music is like a personal story of man experiencing life, love and all the ups and downs self discovery brings.

A.M. Morgan: It's hard to choose one song because Marvin Gaye has an extensive body of work. His love songs are very sentimental, sensual and vividly describe the ups and downs of relationships. One of my personal favorites of his is "Troubled Man." I think I had a false sense of the true nature of men. The song provides a glimpse of how males are reared in terms of the expectations of manhood, especially when it comes to displaying emotions.

6)   Where do you think the belief that men are not supposed to cry stems from? Do you think it's a sign of weakness?

D. Lester Morgan: I think it stems from a male-dominated society. Men are taught not to cry to the point that they actually believe that it is a commandment ordained by God. Crying is therapeutic and has a healing effect.

A.M. Morgan: I agree crying is therapeutic and helps to release all of the pain we often try hard to conceal. No one is immune to heartbreak, disappointment or personal loss. Again, the idea that a man is supposed to be hard and emotionless leaves no room for the reality that he also grieves.

7)   How does who you are as a person reflects who you are as a husband and father?

D. Lester Morgan: Who you are as a person will be reflected in the way you treat your wife and nurture a child. If you tear your wife down, you tear yourself down and it has a negative effect on the nurturing of your child.

A.M. Morgan: That is very insightful. How you are as a person affects the state of all of your personal relationships.

8)   How important is discovering a vocation/calling in life to a man?

D. Lester Morgan: Having been forced to undertake a spiritual journey into self, I realized that I needed a new understanding of what it means to be a man. My indoctrination of manhood was totally misleading. My Aunt Melvina once told me that preachers need to stand before the pulpit and redefine what it means to be a man. I didn't understand that then, but I do now. Any man can father a child, but it takes a strong and committed man to remain in that child's life forever. Manly things don't mean straying away from God and neglecting our responsibilities as men. My vocation has always been working with kids, which is what I was trained to do as an educator. I will spend the rest of my life in pursuit of this vocation.

A.M. Morgan: As a young woman, I was often told that a man is supposed to be strong, intelligent and the backbone of his family. I didn't grasp the concept of his soul-searching or struggling to find his place in society. There is this ideal man that women are conditioned to think exists without being told that he may fall down and have to face some shortcomings before he discovers his true calling. It's funny—a male friend of mine asked, "What do women mean when they say they are searching for a real man?" I honestly couldn't answer that question at the time. The finished product of a well-polished and successful man is something many women desire, but the story of his missteps before he arrived there often falls on deaf ears.

9)   In your opinion, what are five must-haves in a man's repertoire?

D. Lester Morgan: A man must be well-groomed, well-disciplined, well-read, physically and mentally fit, in addition to being spiritually grounded.

A.M. Morgan: I have to agree with your answer. However, I would like to add being respectful. A man desires to be respected, but he must also desire to give that same respect to others.

10) Change is necessary for self-development and for the world to continue to evolve. What makes you uncomfortable about change, and what is your process in learning to embrace it?

D. Lester Morgan: If you don't change, you will find yourself equipped to deal with a world that no longer exists. To become a better person and a better man, I must change starting with the person in the mirror. I sometimes see change around me that looks like we are headed back to old times. Instead of an integrated society, I often see a society where people are still locked out because of color, gender, sexual orientation, wealth, etc., and I don't like it.

A.M. Morgan: Change can be uncomfortable when it involves breaking from a habit that you have grown accustomed to. The hardest lesson I have learned is that I can't make a man be something he is not based on my own agenda or some ultimatum I have given him.

11) Provide some further insight into how a man is influenced by his environment.

D. Lester Morgan: A man is influenced by his environment, but he is also responsible for his own actions.

A.M. Morgan: A man is often judged by his environment, but he is also often trying to change his circumstances to make his life or the life of his family better.

The Gift of Mentoring

One of the greatest secrets of success is having someone to lead and guide an individual in the right direction. A mentor provides a unique perspective to a mentee, with jewels of wisdom on life and its many lessons. A mentor should also be vulnerable enough to share his or her shortcomings in an open and honest dialogue beyond self-judgment. The relationship between mentor and mentee can only flourish when both individuals are willing to go the extra mile to understand each other's true identity. My father has mentored many young males throughout my lifetime. Growing up, I can remember one in particular who would always stop by to pay us a visit. I remember the joy in his eyes because my dad was a father figure to this young man when they initially met in a group home my dad worked. The relationship my dad shared with his mentee inspired me to want to mentor someone because I thought it would be fun and exciting. However, my first mentoring experience taught me that developing a solid relationship of this kind takes hard work and allowing vulnerable moments to occur freely. Overall, to have an enlightening experience a mentor must be willing be appear less than perfect in order to establish a trusting relationship with a mentee.

1) What are the responsibilities of a mentor?

D. Lester Morgan: A mentor should be a good role model and not place himself on a pedestal. The mentee should be taught how he or she arrived at the juncture where he or she is in life. Mentoring requires patience. The mentee doesn't care how much you know until they know how much you care.

A.M. Morgan: A mentor should not try to be invincible. The mentor should recognize that although you may have many life experiences, you will not always have all of the answers to the questions that the mentee has. Learning is a two-way street between a mentor and mentee.

2)   What are some of the most valuable lessons that you learned from one of your first mentoring experiences?

D. Lester Morgan: One of the most valuable lessons that I learned was that it made me a better person. It brought into perspective the many people who were instrumental in my foundation. It reinforced in me the need for mentoring.

A.M. Morgan: A mentee looks up to you for guidance but respects you more when you can share personal experiences in your life. A mentee once told me, "I don't care how successful a person is, if they try to appear perfect I am not listening to anything they have to say." I realized at that moment that I needed be open and honest because it is better appreciated.

3)   What advice can you give to someone who is having a hard time connecting with his or her mentee?

D. Lester Morgan: It takes a lot of perseverance, and sometimes you will doubt yourself. The end result is priceless.

A.M. Morgan: Relationships take a long time to build, and your relationship with your mentee is no different. Once the breakthrough happens between you and your mentee, it will be one of the greatest moments you ever experience.

4)   If you started your own mentoring group, what are the core principles/practices that you would set up to lay the foundation for the program? Why?

D. Lester Morgan: The main core principle would be that if you are going to err, do it in favor of the one you are mentoring. Also, that the group functions as a team. The theory being that I find that many mentors enter a program for the wrong reason or motives. A person should not think of mentoring as something to check off on a to do list. Mentoring is a big commitment just like any other relationship it takes time to develop.

A.M. Morgan: The main core principle would be to foster a positive self-image. I realize as I have gotten older that how I feel about myself is evident in my work ethic, personal relationships and just my attitude in general. The mentoring group would have to practice some type of daily ritual that reinforces the importance of maintaining positive self-images.

5)   What has been one of the funniest experiences between you and a mentee?

D. Lester Morgan: One of the funniest experiences was when one of my mentees introduced me to a woman on an outing. The irony was that he had talked to her and felt that she and I had a lot in common and would be compatible. Overall, this made me realize that my teaching was not in vain.

A.M. Morgan: I hope that was prior to your marriage to mom or it would be time for a serious family discussion. You are something else, and only you could get away with saying something like that. My funniest experience was when my mentee tried to pull a fast one on me. The exchange went something like this: "Let me have five dollars for four ones." I responded by saying, "It would be easier for you to ask me for five dollars than trying to be slick about it." She laughed and informed me that I was smarter than she thought.

6) Is there anyone who you model yourself after as a mentor? If so, why?

D. Lester Morgan: It would take some time for me to name my teachers and mentors. The whole world has mentored me into the person that I am today. I have attempted to abstract the things that are beneficial to me and discard the things that are not. I pay homage to everyone who has played a part.

A.M. Morgan: One mentor in particular that I admire was in Seattle. I was there for five years and the last year was a spiritual hurricane for me. I used to wake up and fall asleep in tears. I did a great job hiding it from everyone but her. I will always appreciate her for allowing me to express my true feelings and not judging me for deciding to quit my job and leave Seattle. She was also a spiritual adviser to me, telling me many ways to find encouragement through biblical references. Overall, in every stage in my life I have always had someone just reach out to me and lend a helping hand, knowledge or wisdom based on their personal experiences.

7) You have worked in several group homes for troubled youth. Most of the youth have trust issues, and it's hard to maintain respect in relationships with them. How were you able to establish connections with these youth? What advice can you give someone interested in helping troubled youth?

D. Lester Morgan: You command respect by being an example for them to emulate. Young people don't care how much you know until they know how much you care. They long for the basic necessity of love. I have never dealt with a child in a way that made him feel emasculated. If you make him feel bad, ensure that he doesn't go to bed that way. This is a profession that will make you laugh at times and also make you cry. The best advice that I can give anyone interested in this profession is not to prejudge and have an open mind.

A.M. Morgan: I mentored and was a substitute teacher in several inner city schools, and the students always expressed to me that they just wanted someone in their lives to never give up on them. I actually learned more from the students about myself than I ever imagined. It helps when you are able to share your personal experiences and listen to them without immediate criticism. When you think about it, we all have unhealed wounds from our past, and just because someone is less fortunate than you doesn't mean their voice should be silenced.

8) There are failing public school systems around the country. Brown vs. Board of Education was supposed to help diminish segregated school systems and create educational systems that were equal for all, despite race. We were told that no child would be left behind. What needs to be done to tear down the educational barriers that currently exist?

D. Lester Morgan: No child left behind is good in theory. However, the flight of families and inequality of wealth in inner cities have left public schools in shambles. Along with them went government dollars and resources. Now we have the charter school concept that only accepts high-performing students. This leaves public schools with kids from the lower economic spectrum. I think that with equal amounts of funding and qualified teachers, any child can learn. I recommend that everyone read, "*The Strange Career of Jim Crow.*" It explains what has taken place with education in America.

A.M. Morgan: I was amazed the first time I walked into a classroom as a substitute teacher and all the students didn't have textbooks of their own. Classrooms are overcrowded, and unfortunately there are not enough teachers. Teachers are underpaid and underappreciated. No matter who you are, a teacher or mentor has impacted your life. The value system in America is tilted on its axis where immediate gratification is often glorified more than the value of an education.

9)   What is the greatest lesson someone, or an experience, has taught you about yourself?

D. Lester Morgan: Experience has taught me that the hardest person to conquer is the man in the mirror. At one point in my life, I tried to lean on my own understanding rather than being guided by God. I now believe in the holistic approach to development, and spirituality has to be a part of it. My life is now in balance.

A.M. Morgan: I recall my first mentoring experience as an adult and the high school students who would teach me more then I could ever imagine. It was the first group gathering with the students in a weekend full of both physical and team-building exercises. The trust fall was an exercise in which everyone climbed to the top of a platform and fell backward in the arms of fellow teammates. I climbed to the top of the platform, but I couldn't gather the courage to let go and trust that my teammates would catch me. When I did not complete the trust fall, I felt really bad, but I had to let go of my pride, step down and face the students, my team and the other mentors. As I stepped down from the ladder, my first thought was, "What will these students think of me and how much of a disappointment am I?" From that point onward, I decided I would fully participate in the other exercises even though I was scared out of my mind. Back in the course room, there was some discussion about the lessons learned throughout the obstacle courses. I was shocked when one of the students said that he wanted to acknowledge the fact that even though I did not complete the trust fall, I did everything else. He said it taught him that even though you can't do some things, there are other things that you can do if you push yourself. Throughout the year, all the students, including the one I mentored, taught me valuable lessons. I learned that my fear of being vulnerable was one of my weaknesses. I now understand that being independent does not need to be a twenty four hour occasion, and allowing someone to step in and help is a big accomplishment for me in the area of trust.

Exploring Hurricane Katrina

The decision to stay home after hearing that Hurricane Katrina was downgraded to a category three storm didn't seem like a big deal for my parents and other local residents. Over the years, many storms had threatened the city of New Orleans and most turned out to be false alarms. I remember speaking to my mother the morning after the eye of the storm had passed. She was in delightfully good spirits, saying that Hurricane Katrina was over and that everything was okay and back to normal. Approximately two hours later, she called in a panicked voice saying, "We have to get out of here," and then the phone disconnected. I was at work at the time and couldn't concentrate due to worry and concern over what exactly was going on. Eventually, I found out that the levees had breached sending overwhelming storm surges into New Orleans and the surrounding parishes. My parents decided to head for Houston, Texas, to stay with some relatives, and it would be several months before any chance of returning to New Orleans was possible. We all returned for the first time in October 2005, feeling as if the soul of the city had disappeared. As we drove by the Superdome on the way home, I felt complete uneasiness in the pit of my stomach. I recalled the horrifying images of hopeless faces, heat exhaustion, hunger and mental anguish that were broadcast on the news and in various media outlets showing residents waiting to be rescued out of the city. I could not believe what I was seeing with my own eyes—the devastating effects of a hurricane on the city known as the Big Easy had left it a lifeless ghost town. My parents are currently living in New Orleans in the same home that I grew up in. My parents are very fortunate to have had minimal damage to their home. However, the day-to-day reality of living in the city post Hurricane Katrina proves just how much New Orleans has changed. Overall, maintaining its cultural essence is still valuable to natives of the Big Easy.

1)   What is it about New Orleans that makes it so special to you? Has the city lost its appeal since Hurricane Katrina?

D. Lester Morgan: New Orleans is very unique as well as a strange fruit. The city can at times make you feel very proud and at times make you feel disgust. It espouses its beauty to the world and its underside goes unnoticed or not talked about. Hurricane Katrina exposed the inequality of wealth in the city. Ironically, the hearts of the power brokers have not changed, and many people remain destitute. The city has not lost its appeal since Hurricane Katrina. The curiosity of tourists still brings them in large numbers and there are still misconceptions about its natives. Its culture is unmatched in the world.

A.M. Morgan: New Orleans is my birthplace and where I was nurtured in my love for the performing arts and where my creativity was born. It is a city like no other in that it welcomes everyone who visits as if they have always lived there. New Orleans has not lost its appeal since Hurricane Katrina; there are so many festivals and cultural events that people from around the world come to visit the city that never sleeps. There is also a stigma surrounding New Orleans, which is negatively portrayed for its shortcomings, but like anything, you don't truly understand something until you experience it for yourself.

2)   Many of the residents, including you and Mom, were still in New Orleans the morning after Hurricane Katrina made landfall. What made you all finally decide to leave?

D. Lester Morgan: I slept through Hurricane Katrina and awakened to a sense of calm because there was no damage in our neighborhood. However, your mom and I kept monitoring the storm by radio telecast. Garland Robinette, a radio personality, said that the levees had been breached and that there would be 20-foot tidal waves. He informed anyone remaining that it was their last chance to evacuate and the only route left was by way of Tchoupitoulas Street and then the Crescent City Connection. We immediately jumped in the car and headed west. There was no one on the highway, and we avoided the massive traffic jams. We arrived in Baton Rouge only to find that the lights were off, so we headed to Houston where we remained for a few months before returning home.

A.M. Morgan: I was in Seattle at the time and was receiving many conflicting stories about what was really going on. Mom called and said you both were alright and then called back and said it was a state of emergency and that you had to leave. The phone disconnected and I could not get through to anyone. I was at work trying to keep my composure, and I lost it and had to go to the restroom to pull myself together. Your niece eventually e-mailed me and said that you were on your way to Baton Rouge. I kept praying for your safety and was so relieved when you both made it to Houston.

3)   What did you miss the most about New Orleans while you where temporarily relocated outside of the city?

D. Lester Morgan: I missed the friendly atmosphere and the close proximity of things. You can travel anywhere in the span of thirty minutes. The people of Houston held a lot of resentment toward the evacuees that was sensationalized by the media. Some concerns were well-founded but most were manufactured.

A.M. Morgan: I haven't lived in New Orleans since I graduated from college in 2001. However, I often miss my family, the southern hospitality, cultural aesthetics and, most notably, the cuisine. I lived in Houston the year after Hurricane Katrina and could sense that the welcoming party for residents of New Orleans slowly coming to an end. Goodwill was replaced with anger over a perceived increase in crime and there was a general attitude that temporary housing for evacuees needed to end. Overall, I thought it was unfair to be labeled as a troublemaker simply for being from New Orleans.

4)   Months after Hurricane Katrina, we went back to New Orleans for the first time and it was like a ghost town. How would you describe that initial experience?

D. Lester Morgan: It brought back not-so-pleasant memories of my military experience, and it appeared to be a third-world country run by the military. I questioned in my mind whether or not we should return. However, finding that we suffered no damage to our house was great consolation and a blessing.

A.M. Morgan: I am so thankful to God there was no severe damage to the place we call home. I must admit that when we first drove into the city it was a ghost town where you could hear yourself breathing because there were no sounds of people or cars.

5)   Hurricane Katrina was more than a physical hurricane; it was also a spiritual one. What has been the impact on your family and friends since the storm?

D. Lester Morgan: Hurricane Katrina made me reassess my life personally. Many lives were lost in the spur of the moment, and the impact is still being felt. One must learn to embrace success as well as tragedy with humility. Unfortunately, there are still many here whose hearts are still hardened, and they are still playing the blame game rather than moving on.

A.M. Morgan: Well, from you and Mom I sensed a bit of frustration in dealing with The Road Home and finding the basic necessities because there weren't many stores opened the first couple of months after you returned to the city. My childhood friends have scattered all over the world since relocating after the storm. Most of them have expressed how much they miss New Orleans and how easy it was to get from place to place. For a lot of people, it felt like they were abandoned by their government and they were angry about the uncertainty of their livelihoods. You can sense hopelessness in the eyes of people realizing that material things have no value when they are washed away in a natural disaster.

6) What positive changes do you see happening for New Orleans in years to come?

D. Lester Morgan: One of the positive changes is in the neighborhoods. All of the remaining houses are newly renovated. Some of the old architecture has made way to new designs. Opportunity for home ownership has increased.

A.M. Morgan: The renovations in the city are great. New Orleans will continue to become a cultural center as more businesses and events come to the city.

7)   Where is your favorite place to visit in the city? Why?

D. Lester Morgan: My favorite place to visit is Waldenburg Park at the river. There is a degree of solitude watching the boats pass along with the different sounds. You also meet a lot of interesting people.

A.M. Morgan: My favorite place to visit is Audubon Park. I enjoy walking the trail when we spend time as a family, just talking about anything that comes to mind. I also remember as a kid you used to take me to Harrell Park where you would run around the track while I would walk. For me, it's all about spending time with my family. I grew up an only child so I really didn't have the sibling experience—you and mom are everything to me.

8)   What is your favorite New Orleans festival or event? Why?

D. Lester Morgan: My favorite event is Mardi Gras. I can honestly say that the experience is unequaled and one to remember.

A.M. Morgan: Big or small, my favorite is any festival or event involving the sound of local New Orleans musicians. I didn't realize how much my life was impacted by music until I started to notice how much I use musical influences to describe integral moments of my life.

The Value of an Education

Everything should be relatively easy because common sense should tell you how to make the best decisions. Well, things are not that simple when lack of education, expertise or experience leads you elsewhere. Graduate from college, get a good job, become a high-achiever and this will guarantee you a promotion, but as in everything there are exceptions to the norm. There are also efficient ways to navigate through your career, but what if you haven't discovered them yet? Success is measured by the quality of the things you produce, but often there is a struggle before the glory of achieving quantifiable results. This is the reality of the real world that no particular college or prep course may have prepared you for. Overall, the value of an education is that it opens doors to opportunities for success, but it is not an entitlement to anything without the hard work and determination to fuel it.

1) What does an education mean to you?

D. Lester Morgan: My mother once said, "Knowledge is something you are born with, and education is something you acquire." Education has fine-tuned my skills and allowed me to be a free thinker. I can research anything that I desire and draw my own conclusions.

A.M. Morgan: Education is an extension of the trained knowledge to do something. I love learning—it is so refreshing to be enlightened about a particular subject, especially when it can be used to empower people.

2) What did you study in college and why? What did you wish to accomplish with this degree?

D. Lester Morgan: I majored in English, Secondary Education and History as a minor. My early motivation was when I heard others say that black people could not be taught Standard

English. I studied history because I knew if one does not learn from the past, he or she is apt to repeat the same mistakes. None of this mattered when I reached the classroom; the need was so great beyond the curriculum that I fell in love with the challenge and the opportunity to make a difference.

A.M. Morgan: I majored in Engineering. I always did pretty well in the math and sciences. I am very analytical while still creative at the same time. One moment I am completely structured in my thinking and in the next I am completely outside of the box of conventional thinking, especially in my writing. One day I would like to teach classes in creative writing. I really enjoy engaging with people and helping them to discover their creative side.

3)   What do you remember most about your college experience? What was your first college roommate like?

D. Lester Morgan: I entered college during the turbulent years of the sixties. During my freshman year, there were protests and demonstrations. The war in Vietnam had just escalated, and there was a lot of civil unrest. My first experience with a roommate remains vivid in my mind and was not a pleasant one. He infringed upon my personal space by borrowing my stuff without permission and allowing others into the room. There were many heated discussions, but we persevered.

A.M. Morgan: I entered college as a freshman and only child. I really never had to share my personal space with someone. My first college roommate had three siblings and she was the oldest.

The first few months of our living arrangements were a bit rocky because I had to grasp the concept of our room instead of my room. She turned out to be a good friend of mine. Her family welcomed me with open arms into their homes and holiday celebrations. I remember that I stopped going to class and wasn't doing well in school, and she called you and Mom. I was upset with her for calling my parents, but it was a phone call that saved my college career. College is where I matured from a young naive girl to a young woman awaiting a whole new world outside of the classroom.

4)   What opportunities has an education provided for you?

D. Lester Morgan: An education has allowed me to travel extensively and interact with people beyond my imagination. Job-wise, I have come full circle from the classroom, human services, corporate America, city government and as an entrepreneur. The value of an education can never be taken away.

A.M. Morgan: I would say the same in regards to an education allowing me to travel and interact with people from various cultures and backgrounds. I have also learned that education does not erase the struggles that come along with just living. A degree shouldn't define who you are—it should complement you as a person. Overall, educating one's self should never end because as time changes, so does the world.

5) What is something that you would like to learn about outside of your skill set? Why?

D. Lester Morgan: I plan on teaching myself several foreign languages. Currently, I am becoming more fluent in French and Spanish. With the ever-changing world, this will be a plus because I plan on traveling the world over during retirement.

A.M. Morgan: I would say learning how to play a musical instrument. I cannot sing, but I love music. I think the piano would be my first effort at learning how to identify and play musical notes. I would definitely like to embark on the journey into songwriting—and let someone else sing the songs, of course.

6) What did you learn from your student-teaching experience that was eye-opening?

D. Lester Morgan: I learned that students don't care how much you know until they know how much you care. The family needs were so great that it affected their work in the classroom. It made me realize that you have to teach beyond what the course requires.

A.M. Morgan: My experience as a substitute teacher taught me that if you can remember the students' names, they really start to listen to you. It is hard to command attention in a classroom, and no textbook reading can prepare you for how the students will react to you. The students can really read your body language well. Respect is a two-way street in a classroom, and it is definitely something that is earned and not granted immediately.

7)   What issues in education are of greatest concern to you? Why?

D. Lester Morgan: Buildings don't teach, teachers teach. The whole mind-set nowadays is to have nice school buildings where no learning actually takes place. With the mass exodus from the inner cities, resources are gone also. It leaves the ones that need the most in segregated classrooms with no hope for a better future. I personally think that it is criminal, and someone should be held accountable.

A.M. Morgan: Equality of resources is definitely a huge concern especially, in the inner cities. It is mind-boggling that in this day and age there are not enough books for every student in some schools. This is critical because some students need to study more outside of school to fully grasp a particular subject. If the student does not have a book to take home, how will he or she ever catch up?

8)   You notice a significant behavior change in a student. What action would you take?

D. Lester Morgan: The first thing that I would do is have a one-on-one teaching interaction with the student. At that point, I would identify the behavior using a statement of empathy. Once the student responds, I will know my next course of action.

A.M. Morgan: The first thing I would do is set up a one-on-one informal discussion with the student. The dialogue would be engaging, and I would not try to diagnose the student and impose my viewpoints. It is very important that the student is able to openly voice concerns if they are willing to do so. If this one-on-

one discussion does not appear to have resolved the behavior changes in the student, then I would recommend setting up an appointment with the school counselor. Overall, if none of this appears to work, then it's time for a parent-teacher conference.

9) Describe your typical teaching style and techniques used.

D. Lester Morgan: My typical teaching style is to lecture and randomly ask questions to the students. It is not uncommon for me to provide an exercise where a student has the floor.

A.M. Morgan: I prefer call and response. I enjoy engaging interactions and getting all of the students involved. It helps to recap what was learned from a previous study lesson as well as an excellent learning tool when it comes to memorization techniques.

10) What is the biggest difference in teaching students in a classroom verses your experiences with providing guidance to children in group homes?

D. Lester Morgan: Usually in the classroom there are fewer behavior problems than in the group home. However, in the group home there are fewer children to staff. Nevertheless, the focus is the same: correct problem behaviors and present an atmosphere that is conducive to learning.

A.M. Morgan: I have never worked in a group home so I don't share that perspective with you. However, as I have mentored and interacted with students in a classroom, it is amazing how much behavior problems are linked to unresolved issues of anger and resentment. Even as adults, how we interact in personal and professional relationships is influenced by good or bad experiences from the past.

11) What is something that you learned in the real world that was never taught to you inside of a classroom?

D. Lester Morgan: I learned that you can be as skilled as you want to be, but at some point you may be out-classed by your opponent.

A.M. Morgan: I learned that it's okay to say I don't know. Don't pretend that you know something that you really don't. There is such a thing as overconfidence.

12) Based on what you know about life from your personal experiences, what would have been most beneficial for you to know as a young person?

D. Lester Morgan: I regret that I was not educated more in industrial skills and taught the benefits of working with one's hands and ownership. In today's society, it definitely would be a plus.

A.M. Morgan: Your words echo a lot of what I learned about Booker T. Washington and in reading *Up from Slavery* while attending Tuskegee. Washington once said, "As long as man knows how to use his hands, he will never be unemployed."

Love and Marriage

Learning to accept someone for who they are is often easier said than done. There are men who often look for the superwoman. A woman who is beautiful, intelligent, submissive yet independent, nurturing, caring and who can be all things at all times. There are women who often look for men who are like prince charming, handsome, rich, powerful, romantic, slightly sensitive and very attentive to her wants and needs. There is a small problem in all of this: Realistically, no one person can be all these things and what happens naturally is disappointment due to unfulfilled expectations. One question should come to mind as one seeks happiness or validation in a relationship: "Do I know and accept who I am?" The truth is quite frankly no person can provide the self-esteem boost that the other person is lacking. The bigger picture in all of this is the disheartening reality that many people seek validation through many external things. The belief that if a person could change x, y or z about themselves then everything would be better is like setting up a recipe for disaster. The reality is if a person changes to please someone else, there is a possibility that the other person could still be unhappy. Finding that special someone to share hopes, wishes and dreams within the union of marriage can become a challenging task. The question each person must ask before entering marriage is, "Am I ready for love and not just the idea of being in love?" This question must be answered or a person may find themselves living unhappily ever after.

1) What is your advice to me on finding love, and how will I really know if a guy is interested beyond something physical?

D. Lester Morgan: Don't go through life with blinders on and don't worry about the biological clock. Remember, the ideal guy is not always the guy with the three-piece suit. If a guy is really interested, you will know. Rise above emotions into the thinking of God.

A.M. Morgan: Come on, you have to admit the guy in the suit is very appeasing to the eye. You know, we initially see with our eyes before our hearts. Seriously, I completely understand where you are coming from. As I get older and remain unmarried people often say to me, "What's wrong with you? Why are you not married?" I think if marriage is a part of my destiny it will happen, but not when I think it should happen or based on some biological clock I think is ticking away from my favor.

2) What are the some of the qualities that I should look for in a potential husband?

D. Lester Morgan: 1) Good listener—will open doors to communication and intimacy. 2) Handy—takes action to solve problems. 3) Provision-oriented. 4) Humility—sensitive and favorable to change. 5) Faithfulness—must be loyal and realize that he is in for the long haul.

A.M. Morgan: Great advice. I am sure all those things take time to develop, especially when two people join together as one in the union of marriage. Someone once told me that I shouldn't try to dictate to a man what he should be. If you constantly question his manhood, he will never respect the relationship—even before you get married. I am not saying you should never challenge a man, but definitely don't try to make him feel inadequate.

3) What do you think will be the biggest challenge for me in marriage? What are your recommendations for overcoming that challenge?

D. Lester Morgan: I think that your independent nature and firm convictions will be your greatest challenge. Having been born an only child, I realize that you were reared that way. However, to overcome that, you must come to the conclusion that there is no "I" in "team." Once married, you must realize that you did not marry family or friends. When confronted with a crisis, consult with an independent counselor or your pastor. Above all, pray.

A.M. Morgan: I must admit I have the hardest time allowing someone else to do things for me. There have been several occasions in my life when I should have asked for help long before I did, and in some cases I didn't ask at all. In regard to my independent nature, I once went out to dinner with a guy and when the check came I reached for it. I didn't do it because I was trying to insult him. I actually thought this time it would be on me. To make a long story short, he was deeply offended and I was like, wow. It was the first time I thought about how that could be interpreted from a male point of view. I have seriously been evaluating several aspects of my character, and I am learning more about myself every day. Marriage is serious business and you are right, there is no "I" in "team."

4) It's often said that women fall more easily in love while men fall less often but more deeply in love. Do you agree or disagree with this statement and why?

D. Lester Morgan: I disagree. I see it in both ends of the spectrum. Men may not admit it as often. Love is a strange emotion. Love/hate relations occur every day.

A.M. Morgan: Well, my female counterparts would say it appears they fall more often. However, as you mentioned, it may be that men do not admit it as often.

5)   What do you think is the worst thing a man can hear from a woman he loves?

D. Lester Morgan: The worst thing that a man can hear from a woman he loves is that she has been unfaithful. I think that once trust has been shattered, it will never be the same. One may forgive, but I don't think it will ever be forgotten.

A.M. Morgan: You know, it's often said women are more forgiving when it comes to infidelity. However, as you mentioned, one may forgive but the offense is never forgotten. Once a bond of trust is broken, it is very hard to rebuild again.

6)   What were you taught were the qualities you should look for in a wife? What made you choose Mom as your wife?

D. Lester Morgan: Being the only boy with three sisters, I was taught that a woman should be gentle. I used to bring young ladies that I dated to the house and let them be evaluated by Mom, Dad and my three sisters without them having any knowledge of my plan. They all were sold on your mom so I made that choice.

A.M. Morgan: Great choice because I am here as a result of the union. Seriously, that says a lot about your character, having your family involved in your decision process.

7)   Name something that brings you joy but sometimes causes you some pain.

D. Lester Morgan: Marriage life brings me a lot of joy but at times it brings about pain. Sharing one's life is a never-ending process. The end result is priceless.

A.M. Morgan: I have never been married so I can't speak from that point of view. However, I do know the things that you love the most will sometimes hurt you. This is why it is important to love without a limit. Unconditional love means accepting someone at their best and worst.

8) What is the difference between whom a man dates verses marries?

D. Lester Morgan: When a man dates a woman, there is always a trap door from which he may escape with no commitment and be easily forgotten. The woman a man marries is the one he brings home to meet his mother and father for their approval. One cannot escape the confines of marriage without learning a valuable lesson that lasts for a lifetime.

A.M. Morgan: The biggest thing I have heard is that a man wants someone who can challenge him to become better. You are right when you say that a man will not take just anyone home to meet his mother and father. Biblically speaking, a wife is a helpmate and nurturer to her husband and family.

There is No Place like Home

New Orleans,

In the words of your fellow natives, "Where you at?" I know some say you will always be missed, but for my family you never left. I understand that Hurricane Katrina took a toll on your spirit, but you still manage to live on. I know that you were upset about all the negative press and sometimes felt you never really got a chance to tell your side of the story. I love you, and quite frankly, everyone who grew up in the Big Easy knows there is no place in the world like you. You are so flavorful in food, people and culture; I can stand still on the city's grounds and still be moved creatively. Overall, as the saying goes, there is no place like home.

1) A person's foundation in life starts in the household environment in which they grew up. Describe the importance of this foundation in the development of your personal identity.

D. Lester Morgan: Material things were never a point of contention in our household. My mother expressed the importance of love and the need for us to stick together. To this day, my sisters and I live by this creed. Our love is not predicated by position or title.

A.M. Morgan: The foundation I received while I was growing up set the precedent for me to not define who I am based on external things. I also learned the importance of helping others succeed when I have valuable tools and resources to empower them. I was taught by you and Mom to endure the pressure despite adversity and to always finish what I started, no matter how long it takes.

2) There is an old saying that states there is no place like home. How did you come to discover the truth behind this statement?

D. Lester Morgan: Ralph Ellison once said, "My only shame is that I once was ashamed." At one time, I may have denied my existence. In traveling the world over, I gained a new perspective on life. You always yearn to return to your place of origin. I recall during Hurricane Katrina, outsiders were questioning why anyone would want to return. Home is where the heart is.

A.M. Morgan: I had lived in Seattle for almost five years, and suddenly I realized how much my family and New Orleans meant to me. Hurricane Katrina put things in perspective for me on the importance of the place where you were born and grew up. I can't deny New Orleans or my upbringing—the root of my value system was planted in Louisiana soil.

3) Did your father ever share anything about the environment in which he grew up? Did you ever meet his father? If so, what was it like spending time with him?

D. Lester Morgan: My father grew up during the Depression. Being the oldest, he had to take care of his siblings after the death of his father. I never met my grandfather, and I have no knowledge of him.

A.M. Morgan: Wow, I never realized that you didn't know your dad's father. I didn't know your dad either so it seems we share a common ground that I hadn't realized before. I am learning about your father through these conversations. He sounds like he was a very hardworking and interesting person to know.

4)   Did your parents ever tell you anything about the importance of providing a stable environment for your children? If so, what was their advice to you?

D. Lester Morgan: My parents showed me a stable environment, and to me that was more important than words. On his deathbed, my father told me that your mother was the one to marry.

A.M. Morgan: The importance of always being honest and truthful to your children is what I learned from you and mom. I sometimes thought it was too candid of an approach while I was growing up, but now I know how valuable of an experience it was.

5)   What aspects of your childhood environment do you find are a part of the foundation of your own household?

D. Lester Morgan: I think that the closeness and cohesiveness of our family is the very foundation that was instilled in me as a child.

A.M. Morgan: The biggest thing is leaving work at work. I always appreciated the fact that when I came home, it was family time and not a discussion about what was going on at work. There were a few times when stress from work carried into our home life, but for the most part it was about enjoying time as a family.

6) How did temporarily living outside of the city and state in which you grew up help you to gain a greater appreciation for your upbringing?

D. Lester Morgan: My upbringing taught me to have a respect for people and their differences. It has molded me to be personable and have a zest for life.

A.M. Morgan: My upbringing taught me to never get too successful in thinking I am better than someone less fortunate than I am.

7) Is there anything that you wish you would have seen more of in the household in which you grew up to better prepare you for certain instances in life?

D. Lester Morgan: I wish that I had paid more attention to food preparation by my mother and sisters. Also, my father worked with his hands a lot in the industrial skills. That would be a plus these days since knowing how to build and create things from the ground up is important in times when jobs are scarce.

A.M. Morgan: I wish we were more openly affectionate with each other. We operated in the mode of showing more than telling each other how much we care. It is often implied more than shared, and at times hearing "I love you" is the vitamin C a person needs.

8) Fill in the blank. Home is:

D. Lester Morgan: Home is the basis and the most important aspect holistically for a person's growth and development.

A.M. Morgan: Home is the foundation of a person's character.

9)   Good or bad, what is the most interesting thing someone has ever told you about their childhood environment that has forever changed their outlook on life?

D. Lester Morgan: My roommate at Southern University, who was drafted by the Chicago Cubs, told me some horrid stories of his childhood. He told me those memories made him practice eight hours daily, and at first he was not that good. Overall, his childhood made him practice harder and motivated him to rise above his circumstances.

A.M. Morgan: A friend of mine once said, "I wish my father was there while I was growing up to teach me the qualities of a real man and how to warrant respect." She was in tears as she said this to me. She said she thinks this is one of the reasons she has not had many successful relationships with men.

10) Life is cyclical and sometimes you end up right back where you started. Can you describe a situation or circumstance in which you ended up in the same place you began?

D. Lester Morgan: I started my work with the federal government, and now I am retiring with the city government. Those experiences have allowed me to come full circle. There have been many jobs, people and experiences in-between. I have come to realize that the journey is what makes life worthwhile, not the accomplishments.

A.M. Morgan: I love the South; it is where I was born, raised and educated. However, after college I wanted to leave my humble beginnings and venture outside of the area. After five years in the Pacific Northwest, I desperately wanted to return to the South. The South is where my heart and my childhood memories are. I can't imagine being anywhere else. Now that I am back where I started, I can say I understand that sometimes you have to leave or lose something to appreciate it.

11)   How would you describe the New Orleans dialect?

D. Lester Morgan: The New Orleans dialect is unequaled. It is a mixture of so many races and geographical locations that you scratch your head at times and wonder.

A.M. Morgan: The New Orleans dialect is fun and uses certain inflections to express the spirit of letting the good times roll.

12)   What is your favorite catchphrase that makes you smile and lets you know that it's strictly New Orleans vernacular?

D. Lester Morgan: My favorite catch phrases are "Ya heard me," and "Where you at?" Use those two and you can communicate with anyone here.

A.M. Morgan: One of my favorites is "Where you at?" as it simply means hello. My other personal favorite is "You are smelling yourself." Not sure if it is a New Orleans, Louisiana or Southern phrase. It simply means you are completely conceited and into yourself a bit too much at that particular moment.

13)   Who is your favorite New Orleans musician? Why?

D. Lester Morgan: I would have to say Louis Armstrong. He overcame poverty, a lack of a formal education and racism to become one of the most influential musicians of the twentieth century and world-renowned. Abandoned by his father at the time of his birth, he was raised by his mother in the slums of New Orleans. While incarcerated in a home for wayward boys, he was introduced to the cornet and other musical instruments. He pioneered a style known as swing that formed the basis for most jazz and rhythm and blues. To me that is truly a success story.

A.M. Morgan: I can't narrow this question down. I love several New Orleans musicians for different reasons. I just love the melodies and distinct sounds of New Orleans-style music whether it's jazz, funk or soul.

14)   What family member has been your greatest hero?

D. Lester Morgan: My greatest hero has been my Aunt Melvina, who is currently in her nineties. She and my mother were sisters- I was blessed to have had them both. To this day, she still has the presence of mind where I can have an intellectual conversation with her. Her wisdom, perseverance and understanding have carried me throughout my life. Her Christian ethics and unconditional love will be forever cherished.

A.M. Morgan: I am going to say the family members that were my heroes were my grandmothers. Those two women were very giving without thinking twice about it. I remember attending their funerals and seeing people from all walks of life coming in to pay final respects. My grandmothers taught me that you are never too small or insignificant to make a difference.

15) Louisiana is under fire in the news and media. Historically, the state has always had issues with race matters, questionable practices and corruption in government. Despite the apparent issues that exist in the Pelican State, what seems to be the biggest misconception in the media?

D. Lester Morgan: The biggest misconception is that the politicians are all corrupt, and the people of the state are completely illiterate. Race and the perception of race have always been a point of contention for residents. Hurricane Katrina did not discriminate based on race or economic status. This hurricane disaster cannot be compared to any other based on the sheer magnitude of its devastation.

A.M. Morgan: Louisiana has had trouble with the balance of power for quite some time, but it's not just one state's exclusive issue. I remember seeing a broadcast on CNN calling New Orleans "Murder City, USA," and I felt immediate sadness. Violent crimes and homicides are plaguing the streets of many U.S. cities—not just New Orleans.

16) What would you like your family legacy to be?

D. Lester Morgan: I would like to have my picture displayed on the mantle piece. This would signify that I was an example for all the family to follow and that my works speak for themselves.

A.M. Morgan: I assure you that your picture will be on the mantle piece.

The Road to Forgiveness

On my left hand there is a scar that spans from the inside of my middle finger to just below the knuckle, limiting its mobility. May 1996 was the year I was involved in a domestic dispute between my parents. My father's rage left physical and emotional scars. I can remember that night very vividly, hearing my mother's cries and screams as she ran toward me, hoping that my father would come to grips with the reality of the moment. A few seconds later after a brief struggle, I was in complete shock as a knife sliced into my hand creating a laceration so severe that I almost lost my finger completely. Moments later, I was rushed to an emergency room and taken into surgery. The next thing I remember is waking up in recovery only to discover that my father had been arrested for domestic violence. I would later sign an affidavit to drop all of the charges, but it would take a long time to pick up the pieces in our lives. I went to physical therapy for several months before my freshman year of college; I gained some sensation back, but I am still unable to fully use my left hand. Emotionally, I carried anger for several years after this accident. I couldn't even speak the truth so I would make up a story anytime anyone would ask me about the scar on my hand. This was a burden to my heart as I searched for the answers as to why this happened. I have struggled to understand everything that happened, and it has taken a great level of patience to get through the pain. My father and I had to heal many wounds by discussing all the things that lead to the night of the accident and why so much anger led to uncontrollable rage.

1) May 1996 changed our lives as a family forever. Can you describe what was going on in your life at the time that led you to an uncontrollable fit of rage?

D. Lester Morgan: During this period, your mother and I were having marital problems. Our financial situation at the time only exacerbated the problem. On the night in question we were arguing as to where you would attend college. The argument escalated and you were injured when you intervened. It is ironic that we were arguing about something that should have been discussed between the three of us.

A.M. Morgan: I used to listen to the both of you argue all of the time, and inside I would cringe. I hate seeing or hearing people that I love in pain. That night I remember slightly nodding off and hearing Mom scream, "Alicia, help me!" When she ran in the room, I jumped up and I remember not recognizing you because you were like a mad man. You had a knife in your hand, and after I realized my finger was severed I was in complete shock. I hid the incident from everyone who did not know what happened. Every time someone asked what happened to my hand, I lied and told them I accidently cut myself. I was angry with you, but I still wanted to protect your character. I also felt guilty because I knew the argument was about me attending college. Walking across the stage four-and-a-half years later meant more than a college degree—it was more of an appreciation of the sacrifices and grace of God that allowed me to reach that point.

2)   Once you realized the aftermath of that night, how did you come to grips with the course of your actions?

D. Lester Morgan: That night was the darkest time in my life. The depth of my guilt was overwhelming and it consumed me day and night. I came to grips with my actions by acknowledging that I had lost control. I sought solace but none was there. One of my college friends, now a minister, happened to work with me at my job at the time and guided me in gaining a perspective as to what had happened.

A.M. Morgan: I think at this point in my life I am finally coming to grips with what happened that night. I always felt like I was getting the cold shoulder from you in regard to speaking about the events that led to that night. It was like the elephant in the room, and I just wanted closure as to why it happened.

3)   When I awoke from surgery in the recovery room, I was informed that you were arrested. I remember a few years later that you told me that some of the people you saw in the cell with you were people you had previously mentored or helped in group homes. How did you face that experience, and what did you say to them?

D. Lester Morgan: The first person that I met during booking was a young man that I had mentored. He couldn't believe that I had been arrested after all the advice that I had given him. My response to him was that I am no different than any other man. The irony was that he actually counseled me during my short stay. I also knew several officers who expressed disbelief that I was there.

A.M. Morgan: Wow, that must have been quite a double dose of how human and vulnerable you had become at that moment. It takes a great amount of character to admit to those whom you have previously encouraged to do the right thing that you too can fall short and make bad decisions.

4)   For eight years after the accident, I silently harbored anger and resentment toward you. I prayed for the understanding to forgive you. Did you ever sense a distance between us during that time?

D. Lester Morgan: I was dazed during that period. The pain that I felt was real because I did not anesthetize the pain in any way. I want to thank you for not showing your resentment and anger toward me, and I am sure it was difficult. I sensed the distance, but I regarded that as natural. I prayed for understanding and was moved in ways unimaginable. Please forgive me again for my transgression.

A.M. Morgan: I prayed that our relationship would be healed. I was both angry and at a crossroads because I wanted you to feel the pain I was feeling. In my heart I forgave you, but in my mind I struggled to let go of the emotional scars. I cried every time I thought of the accident because when I looked at my hand I had a constant reminder. When you love someone unconditionally, you must accept all aspects of their character, and I didn't quite understand what that meant until this test of our relationship.

5)   What did this ordeal teach you about yourself?

D. Lester Morgan: This ordeal taught me that anyone can reach a breaking point. I always thought that I was in control, but now I realize that one is powerless if they do not seek a higher power.

A.M. Morgan: When something traumatic happens in your life, it affects how you deal with your personal relationships. Every time I sense an argument happening, I fear that it will end in a bad way. For this reason, I have often avoided conflicts. I know that this is not a good way to keep the lines of communication open, but I understand that because of the accident a part of me is afraid that it could happen again.

6) Do you think any unresolved issues of your past have adversely affected the health of your personal relationships? If so, in what aspect?

D. Lester Morgan: I think that I allowed my family to make a decision as to whom I would marry and that decision should have rested with me alone.

A.M. Morgan: As I mentioned earlier, I think the fear of being vulnerable has affected the success of my personal relationships. In addition, in our family being openly affectionate was not very common. I have been told I am hard to read because my actions are not always overly expressive. For me, when I love someone I will do everything to make sure I am always there for that person.

7) Do you see any parts of your father in yourself? If so, has this caused any personal struggles for you?

D. Lester Morgan: My father came across as a strict disciplinarian, and maybe I also struggle with wanting to see perfection in others, and that has been a disappointment.

A.M. Morgan: I always felt the pressure from you to be perfect and not show my shortcomings. I resented that about you and thought you were being unfair and unrealistic. No one is perfect so expecting someone to always far exceed your expectations is setting yourself up for disappointment. As far as myself, I have inherited your sense of not showing my emotions. This can be a recipe for disaster if you just let how you really feel build up because you can reach a boiling point.

8) Have you truly forgiven yourself for the accident in May 1996? What is/was your process in doing so?

D. Lester Morgan: I will never forgive myself for the incident. To forgive myself would be to deny that it happened. I have searched spiritually for an answer but found no scripture on forgiving one's self. I try not to dwell on what happened because it still brings a lot of pain.

A.M. Morgan: I have to respectfully disagree. Forgiveness of self is essential in the healing process. It doesn't mean that you forget the course of your actions, but it says that you acknowledge what you have done, sincerely apologize and seek guidance from God on the road to forgiveness. You can't erase your transgressions, but you can make the effort to learn from your mistakes and not repeat them again.

9) It's often been said there is a blessing buried inside of every tragedy. Do you think something positive stemmed from the accident?

D. Lester Morgan: That tragedy made me realize that God will take something or someone away that you love to get you in order. I pray that God will order my steps and not me. It taught me that love sometimes hurts, and you can't tell how much you really love someone until you have to love them in the midst of a painful situation or trying times. Love is truly stronger than pride.

A.M. Morgan: The incident taught me that a person can be your hero but still not be immune to making mistakes. It also taught me to become one with my emotions because it is not something that you can run from forever. I also learned about the ugly side of human nature and how much loving someone is hard in the darkest moments in life.

10) What is your biggest failure in your career, parenting or life? How did you overcome it?

D. Lester Morgan: At one point in my life, I did not live in harmony with myself and God. This manifested itself in me not taking advantages of opportunities. In doing so, I lost concept of time. Nevertheless, I could always hear the elders in the back of my mind saying that I know better. Through prayer and exercise, I was able redirect my life.

A.M. Morgan: My biggest challenge has been in realizing that being who you are means that some will not accept you. I prayed that we would overcome our differences and become a close-knit family again. I now understand that having a point of view sometimes mean disagreeing with others. You spoke of being in harmony with yourself and God; I would say that means I will no longer fight my true self.

Father and Daughter Time Takeaways

The mirror reveals a reflection of a man and woman best described as father and daughter. The image seen is of kindred spirits in a portrait displaying how kind or unkind the effects of human and outside nature can be to a person. The message is clear: The strong bond between A.M. Morgan and D. Lester Morgan is the product of lessons in forgiveness, love, trust and most importantly, the curveballs thrown to test the strength of this family's ties. The only thing that is certain from this point onward is that change is inevitable and you have to let go of the unnecessary need to control the process. This is a great, real-life story that serves as an example to others that trouble lives but does not have to last always. Overall, the road to internal happiness has not been a paved one for this family, and although their hearts have known great sorrow, there are no regrets on their journey to self discovery and forgiveness.

1) What impact has having these conversations and writing this book had on you? Are you afraid that you are exposing too much information about yourself and that it may have a negative impact on other's perception of you?

D. Lester Morgan: I have shared information with you that I have never shared with anyone and vice versa. My reality comes from within, and I leave it at that. If this information empowers you and makes me a better person, then so be it. These conversations have been thought-provoking and therapeutic.

A.M. Morgan: I just have to say thank you again for allowing us to share these conversations. I just had so many questions bottled up inside and this was very therapeutic and eye-opening for me as well. I don't worry about exposing too much of myself and what people will think of me after reading this book. I have learned that at the end of the day, my true colors embody who I am, and anyone unwilling to accept that isn't really someone I can call a friend.

2)   What do you hope that readers will gain from reading this book?

D. Lester Morgan: I hope that readers get the impression that a man can be imperfect yet be a good father. Fatherhood is for life, and I plan on being there for you.

A.M. Morgan: I hope that people are able to see that it is possible to rebuild a relationship even after painful circumstances. Father and Daughter Time is about the conversations that led to an understanding of how unconditional love helped us both conquer our demons.

3)   What are some of your writing goals? What would you like to accomplish after the completion and release of this book?

D. Lester Morgan: My writing goal is to be consistent. I hope that the completion and the release of this book will be a springboard for others to come.

A.M. Morgan: I hope this book helps to further launch both of our writing careers. The sky is the limit, and longevity in the publishing business is our mission.

4) Imagine you are signing the inside cover of this book for someone who has not had a positive relationship with their father but still plans to read it. What would your inscription to them say?

D. Lester Morgan: Only God knows what a person goes through. Write your own success story in life, and do not let the past be a hindrance.

A.M. Morgan: Accept your past but exhibit love for your future by letting its lessons flow freely without letting it define who you are currently.

5) How would you describe the journey to rebuilding our relationship to a healthy one? What are the key steps for restoring broken family bonds?

D. Lester Morgan: The journey has been difficult personally because I still deal with forgiving myself. I thank you for reaching out and for our communication on a daily basis. The key step has been acknowledging my mistakes and behavior along with focusing on the future.

A.M. Morgan: It has been exciting and also eye-opening. I actually discovered the true depth of my emotions while exploring the foundation of who I am. The key step in restoring broken family bonds is stepping down from the pedestal of pride. Pride hinders forgiveness and leaves a person with a heavy heart filled with anger and resentment.

6)   What do you find that is so unique about this book? Describe its importance in today's world.

D. Lester Morgan: This book is unique because the venture has not been for profit but very therapeutic in nature. It is very important in today's world because parents seldom, if ever, communicate on this level of honesty.

A.M. Morgan: This book is unique because it is a candid dialogue between a father and daughter that provides an introspective look on how they view one another. It is not a perfect relationship but proves communication is essential.

7)   Fill in the blank. Father and Daughter Time is:

D. Lester Morgan: Father and Daughter Time is like a refreshing spring that flows endlessly with no bounds.

A.M. Morgan: Father and Daughter Time is like a history lesson in retrospect. It will forever be a trace of our lives together.

8)   Any last words?

D. Lester Morgan: Live every day like it is going to be your last, and continue to learn like you are going to live forever.

A.M. Morgan: It is our hope that we have inspired you to have heart to heart conversations of your own. Thanks for reading this book; your time is greatly appreciated.

ABOUT THE AUTHORS

A.M. Morgan is a native of New Orleans who currently resides in North Dallas Texas. She is a graduate of Tuskegee University with a Bachelor's of Science Degree in Aerospace Science Engineering and New Mexico State University with a Master's of Science Degree in Industrial Engineering with a Manufacturing Minor. She is a lover of words and a creative spirit who also enjoys participating in the performing arts. Visit www.ammorgan.net to find out more about A.M. Morgan

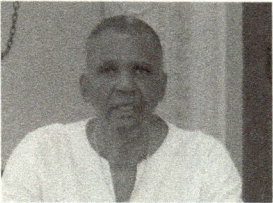

D. Lester Morgan is a Slidell Louisiana native who is a country boy at heart who enjoys living the simple life. He believes that in order to develop holistically one has to be mentally and physically fit. As part of that development he reads regularly and runs 5-10 miles daily. He received a Bachelor's of Arts Degree in Secondary Education with a History Minor from Southern University in Baton Rouge, Louisiana. His favorite quote is, "It's not how long you live but the quality of life that you have while you are here." He currently resides in New Orleans.